SOCIAL SHER'S

THE SKILLS
THAT PAY THE BILLS

SOCIAL SHER'S

THE SKILLS
THAT PAY THE BILLS

STAN SHER

CONTENTS

ACKNOWLEDGEMENT

To write a book, especially a first one, has been a journey that brought fulfillment and a feeling of self-accomplishment. I want to start this off by showing my appreciation to all the people that inspired me throughout my life and helped me get this book completed in the best form possible. It has not been possible without the life experiences I have participated in to get this far (and we are just getting started, my friends).

I have to start by paying tribute to my immediate fallen heroes, beginning from my grandfather Matvey Sher, a true family leader. This man was hit by a motor vehicle in Ukraine and spent the second half of his life disabled on crutches. However, he never gave up on life and was one of the strongest men I ever knew. For five years, he walked two miles on his crutches every day to pick me up from school, and we walked back together for two miles. My grandmother Bina raised me after school and helped me develop into a grown-up early, as you will read later in this book. They were my grandparents on my father's side of the family. I was the sunshine of their life, and they were the best grandparents that a person could have. Sadly both have passed away but will remain in my heart forever.

I want to pay tribute to my father, Alexander Sher. My father was my everything! My immediate memory comes from remembering how he fought for me when I was bullied as a kid by not only other kids but also the school system that tried to bring me down. I remember so many instances when that man came to my rescue. As I got older and started developing career success, we did not always agree about things, but he never judged me. My father believed in every move I made because he saw how far I was going. My dad loved watching me speak in public and used to get blown away by how much better I kept getting. I still cannot believe that it is only less than two years since he passed.

I want to give my love and tribute to my mother, who is currently suffering many health problems. She is a three-year stroke survivor and a diabetic. It was challenging after my dad passed away as I managed two households and got her the best care I could afford. I love my mother and will always be here for her. My immediate family is super small, and aside from a grandfather, aunt, and two cousins, and my fiancé, other than having a lot of really close friends. I want to thank Karina, Samuel, Daniel, Ben, and my grandfather Eugene (the immediate family) for always admiring my actions.

My fiancé, Jennifer Siegmann, needs her own paragraph. I had never indeed known what love is until I met you. From the first time we met, I knew she was special and somehow going to end up with me. In the time we have been together, we developed an unbreakable bond. We saved each other in various ways. She is the editor of this book and has dedicated as much time as I did writing it. This is truly a team effort, and she is my partner in life and business. They say that behind every great man is a great woman. My love, Jennifer makes that statement true!

I want to thank the people mentioned in this book in the chapters to come for believing in me and allowing me to step up. Every experience in life is supposed to give us tools that will better ourselves. A special thank you goes out to our "godfather of automotive digital marketing," Ralph Paglia, a legend in the automotive industry. He taught me how to become the jack of all trades and the importance of gaining knowledge and experience to fit in anywhere in the business world. Lastly, thank you, my reader, for taking the first step to being inspired to grow.

CHAPTER 1

STARTING FROM THE BOTTOM

My name is Stan Sher, and first, I want to thank you for investing your time in reading my book. I specifically wrote this with the purpose of sharing my story to increase your motivation and inspire you to strive to become successful in this journey that we call life. This book will have many different meanings and may come off to some as a heartwarming motivational book, while others will see it as a business and marketing tool. I genuinely want to break the existing structural barriers and write what is in my heart! So with that, let's begin this adventure.

Something that I recently experienced during this rough year of 2020 is "life is way too short." As I write this, I am thirty-eight years old, living in the most troubled times that our world has ever experienced. We are enduring an immeasurable pandemic with the Covid-19 virus moving across the globe. We are experiencing a lot of negativity in this world because, at every turn, our media surrounds us with negative propaganda. But that is not what profoundly hurts me, as it is not something that I can control!

Sadly, I lost a piece of my heart this year. My father passed away at age sixty-one due to liver cancer. What's worse is that we lost him in less than ninety days of finding out that he had this terminal disease. This amazing man lost his life and never got to experience all the happiness that a person in their sixties deserves to enjoy. At the same time, I settled down with the love of my life and my purpose for continuing to stay strong, my fiancé Jennifer. My father never even got the chance to meet her.

He lost his life after working hard for many years and supporting himself and my mother, who also got sick over two years ago after surviving a stroke. My parents lived in the lower middle class their entire life, trying to make ends meet while carrying on old school traditions and beliefs. They never read a motivational book, and they never surrounded themselves with highly successful people. They never took any risks, such as taking their last 1,000 dollars and investing it in flying across the country to attend an industry conference to network and look for better career paths. When I would take such bold risks, I was looked down on, often catching criticism. However, my father understood that I was going to make it and appreciated my tenacity. The first time I got published in an automotive industry magazine, he realized I was on my way to making it.

It all goes back to me being a child. When we would fix something at home or need to use tools, I was almost completely incapable. But my father, on the other hand, was a sewing machine mechanic before becoming an automobile mechanic. We come from a family of machinists, which included my grandfather and my grandfather's brother. My father's words were always, "son, if you need to make a living, don't get your hands dirty and bruised. I want to see you wearing suits and ties, not dirt and grime". I cannot repair many things when they break, but I can afford to get them fixed. Now, my mother was a music teacher and manicurist when she was at the top of her game, working at one of the most upscale salons in

New York City. Unfortunately, the stroke she suffered has seriously limited her abilities as of late.

By my own choice, I started working at the young age of fourteen. My parents raised me very well, and I am fortunate to say that I never gave them any issues growing up. I believe that spending my early years with my Eastern European grandparents after school taught me values early. I always completed my homework right after school, and I stayed out of trouble. By age eleven, I came home after school, finished my chores and reading, I even cooked food without burning down the house. By the way, I was home alone for five hours while both parents were still at work. I became a very responsible and independent young man.

I guess you can say that I grew up way too fast. I learned quickly about culture shock and the hard way through. In our first five years living in the United States, we lived in Brooklyn, NY. I got into martial arts at a really young age and became a fan of the Mighty Morphin Power Rangers. It seemed like many kids my age were fans. We moved to East Brunswick, NJ., and I realized what was trendy in New York for some reason is not out here. In fifth grade, I wore a space ranger costume for Halloween, and I got bullied for it for a few years. I moved into a different world and needed to adjust.

In fact, I was very different from everyone else, and I got pushed around for a few years. But one thing that my tormentors could never do was hurt me. I remember vividly how once in the sixth grade, my school bus dropped us off, and as we got off, I got attacked by not one or two but five kids. This is a true story. Sometimes I wish there was a camera rolling for this conflict. It was as exciting as a fight scene in a movie.

All five bullies took me on, and all five ended up getting their asses handed to them. I used the edge of an umbrella to handle my biggest bully while I flipped one over me. They all ended up on the ground, and I know that if a parent did not stop this, someone would have ended up in the hospital. I had grown tired of all of the bullying, and at the point, it became life or death for me, I had to move on.

Those challenges were just something that I endured in my early years. I started making friends in high school, and a select few remain my ride-or-die friends to this day. As we all got older, we began to see each other for the positive energy that we brought around us. This was my first realization where I understood the importance of being an ethical human being.

How about more adversity?

I had a hard time adjusting to my school curriculum and ended up in the special education program. I was so embarrassed that I worked for three years (grades 6-8) to get out, working on a new subject every year. It started with math in sixth grade to history in seventh grade, and finally English in eighth grade. By high school, I fitted in with everyone else. I learned a lesson in goal setting and how the struggle to grow was real, and I made it!

I started working at fourteen years old by my own choice. My parents raised me very well, and I am fortunate to say that I never gave my parents problems. I believe that spending my early years with my Eastern European grandparents after school taught me values early. My homework was always done right after school, and I stayed out of trouble. By age eleven, I came home after school, got my chores and homework done, and cooked food without burning down the house. By the way, I was home alone for five hours while both parents were at work.

Once I started working in the summer I started creating goals for myself. I went to work for a successful pool management company as a lifeguard. I was not just any lifeguard though. My parents gave me permission to work long hours and actually develop a serious work ethic. When I say I worked long hours I mean I actually worked sixty hour weeks and took only one day off every week. While the average teenager made $2,000-3,000 per summer I was making $7,000 per summer by age sixteen.

The lifeguard instructor that certified me also became a mentor and lifelong best friend. His name is Gabriel Lotesto, and I am honored to have had him in my corner. This man never gave up on me, and together we did some incredible things at this job. I worked for that company for seven years.

Every achievement in my life had to come from blood, sweat, and tears. For example, I was terrible at taking tests. The first summer I went to work, I failed the written portion of my Lifeguard and CPR certification. I passed the physical part without problems. This prevented me from working more hours and kept me working as a badge checker for that initial summer. I had the same trouble getting my driver's license too. I passed the driving test quickly but had to take the written test three times. Was it a learning disability, or was it just a major flaw in my mind? I will never know. I know that eventually, I became one of the best lifeguards in the company, and I also became a great driver.

I had test-taking issues in school too. My grades were not the best, but I grasped concepts and learned a lot of what I studied. Other things that I was not great at were wrestling. I was competitive and wrestled for six years until I finished high school. I did not win many matches, but it kept me in shape and gave me striving goals. The two things that I was great at were martial arts and playing the guitar.

I practiced martial arts from age nine to twenty. I attained a 2nd level brown sash. At age twelve, I picked up the guitar and immersed myself in it. By age fourteen, I was able to semi-shred. Some parts came naturally to me, while others are still difficult to this day. I will never be Eddie Van Halen or Steve Vai, but I will always play in my style to blow off some steam and have fun in my bedroom.

It all boils down to the fact that I was always self-aware and understood my direction. Life was moving fast, and I needed to grow up quickly, so I formulated plans for my path. I grew up in an affluent town where many of my friends and classmates drove new cars to school while driving a thirteen-year-old Toyota Camry. But the facts are my parents could not afford a more expensive vehicle for me. My parents did not even have a college fund set up for me. They did, however, always get me what I earned and what I needed. I am proud to say I was never spoiled.

I wanted a brand new car like my friends, so I worked for it. Every summer between the ages of fifteen and twenty-one, I worked six days a week, putting in over sixty hours as a lifeguard and a swim instructor. All I did was stash my money for the future. At nineteen years old, I had $12,000 in the bank and a 740 credit score. I bought my first new car and paid for each semester of college with my own money and no loans. I started to create plans for my future and what I wanted to do for a living. Back in those days, we never used "hustle" as commonly as we do nowadays. But hustling is what I was doing, and I was self-motivated.

Based on my experience working with children and being a professional rescuer, I contemplated the path of becoming a school teacher. In fact, at nineteen years old, I was looking for a job that would require me to start dressing for success. I was considering a career in sales to become a better communicator and fulfill my father's dream of not working with my hands to make a living. Besides, I had zero interest in doing manual labor. But I do respect the professions and people that perform those jobs.

At twenty years old, in my second year of college, my parents decided to move out of New Jersey. They were trying to drag me with them. I said, "nope, I'm a grown-up. I'll make it on my own". I wanted to become self-reliant and, after four months, I blew through my savings and realized I needed a backup career to support me for now until I finish school. So I went on the hunt for better opportunities. I got hired to sell "Life Alert" over the phone only to be fired and told that I would not make it, just two days after being hired. I had to face facts and try face-to-face sales.

What a great idea this was.

Enter the car business.

I responded to an ad to sell cars. I wore pants and a dress shirt to the interview, and I only got hired because I had a pulse. They put me through two weeks of training with a consultant that goes by the name of Hoss Devine. He was old school but effective. It was Hoss that taught me how to tie a tie. On the day he left the dealership, I had to prove myself on a crowded showroom floor. The first customer that I took I sold the very next day. A few hours later, they referred me to their brother, who also bought a car from me. I made over $1000 in commissions and was hooked. Out of the gate, I sold two vehicles, and they cut my tie.

I sold a few more cars, but I was not too fond of the dealership, so I switched jobs, and my experience in moving around the car sales industry started. I was a massive fan of the Honda brand since I drove a Honda Civic. I will tell you, just like with everything else in my life, this would be a difficult path. It took me six months to get to sell 20 cars per month. My confidence lacked for over a year. I was terrible at overcoming objections, and while I was professional and liked by people, I did not truly have "the balls" to ask for the money. They always said, "it's just like talking to a girl and scoring a date." Well, guess what, I was terrible at that too.

The most important part of that experience was the lifelong best friend that I made. We had a finance manager that was a few months older than me. At the dealership's Saturday morning meeting, they told us he just got promoted to finance director. Someone told me he was my age. Here is a man my age with a six-figure director position in charge of a multi-million dollar department. He was twenty-one going on forty-one with the level and experience of how he operated.

I was suddenly inspired and said I wanted to be like him. I quickly made it a point to become friends and learn as much from him as I could. He took me under his wing and mentored me. He even sent me his referral customers to sell. His name is Christopher Haas, and he is one of my lifelong best friends. Throughout the many years to come, we would become family. We have done so much for each other. If it were not for his inspiration, I would not be where I am today!

At the same time, I was going to college and progressively losing interest in becoming a teacher. After all, here I am, making $1,700 a week at 20 years old. My history professor, with his fancy book smarts and significant degree, was doing IT full time for a public library for $500 a week and teaching an adjunct class. I realized that I want to be in a career that will allow me to have a high income so that I can not only live a more fruitful life but also take care of anything and everything for myself and, more importantly, my family.

The lesson here is that we must never give up! I had tutors when I was younger that put in time and energy into me to make sure that I succeeded. My parents spent hard-earned money that they could not afford to help me grow. Life was a struggle, and everything had to be genuinely earned. I knew early on that everything would be a struggle. The only thing that I lacked in those days was confidence. My future growth certainly gave me more than enough.

If others are investing time and resources into you, it is because they believe in you. Take every opportunity to learn and grow from this experience. The way that I see it is that this is the ultimate definition of how to survive and thrive in a challenging world. I never gave up. I implore you never to give up and try harder. Do not be afraid to work more than one job at the same time because it is important to develop the discipline needed to succeed in life.

CHAPTER 2

TAKE CARE OF WHAT'S IMPORTANT

It was time to start taking care of my family. I decided to join my parents in Florida, after almost two years of being on my own in New Jersey. I was twenty-one years old, and I adjusted to living independently and handling my finances. I started to befriend many successful people, and my goals quickly grew. But now it was time to see what I could do since I am now independent but will be living with my parents parents again. This is in a new state where I did not know anyone. I bought my second brand new car just weeks after I moved to Florida. It was a manual transmission Acura RSX. It was a pretty rare vehicle in that area.

Reality sinks in when your family needs your help. I moved in with my parents to figure out life in Florida. Within a few weeks of the move, my father had a triple bypass, and my mother was barely working. My dad was out for two months, and he was not receiving much money to pay the bills, so I helped as much as I could. I was living rent-free, but I always made sure I took care of the expenses. My mom would send me grocery shopping, and I would buy food and never take a penny back. We needed a grill for the backyard, so I bought the best one money can buy.

My family was small, but we took care of each other. If I figured out how to be successful at a young age, I would considerately share it with my loved ones. Still, the mindset of my parents was different from mine. I was not living economically. I never said no to anything. If I wanted something, I would buy it. If my parents felt something was too expensive, no problem, I would take care of it.

So, how were you supposed to start supporting your family in an unfamiliar town with a new job and zero connections?

I developed a social life thanks to AOL and MySpace at the time. We are living in the year 2005 where those were the ways to meet people. I went on many dates and made friends with some local people. It was also a culture shock for me again, but I adjusted.

I jumped right into selling cars. I was already a silver-level council of sales leadership Honda salesperson, so my credentials automatically transferred over. Courtesy Honda, an AutoNation dealership, hired me to be an Internet Sales Manager. As I started five days into the new month, I learned CRM and the art of selling customer's vehicles on the internet. Hitting the ground running, I was selling cars like a madman. My Internet director valued my abilities and even started feeding me his referrals to help me boost my volume.

That first month even with the missing five days, I sold and delivered twenty-five units. However, I got beat out for salesman of the month by a ten-year veteran by just one unit. Losing was an eye-opening experience for me. Still, I was just about to turn twenty-two years old, and I made $10,000 that month. That was a game-changing moment for my career. I was hungry, and I wanted more, so I continued my over twenty cars a month streak.

Now here is where harsh reality sets in on you! I got too confident and started feeling like I was the best. I went on a vacation, came back, and had two of the worst months ever. I had to struggle to sell ten units and only made $2,000 those months. The truth is that even top performers can go through a slump. The way that I got my mindset right again was to go back to the basics and forget about being a "know it all," and I checked my ego at the door.

There were days when I sold four and five units while the whole store only did eight. Our Internet department had six sales professionals delivering over one hundred and twenty units per month. They promoted me to a working manager that was not only selling but also helping close deals for the rest of the team. It was a great job, and it allowed me to support my family and, at the same time, stash money away. It put me in a position where I was ready to buy my first home before turning twenty-three years old.

Speaking of buying my first home, this almost happened because of a fight that I got into with my dad. I was working so many hours and coming home late every night that other than paying for things to help the household, I was not helpful physically at home. One day he and I got into it, and I started packing up my stuff. He said, "where will you go?" to which I replied, "I am going to rent an apartment for a few months and then go buy my own house." I added, "what? You don't think I can afford to buy my own house?"

I got too comfortable being a grown-up at such an early age while many of my friends were finishing up at college that I felt independent. This fight lasted two days, and we mended fences. I had arguments with my dad like this maybe three times in my life, even as a teenager. My father and I were so close that he would never allow me to leave. We were an immediate-knit family and always took care of each other.

But what happened to school?

I did not enroll in college again (at least at that time), and I just focused on my career. I read books and continued to surround myself with successful people. Everyone you meet can be some sort of inspiration to grow and better yourself. Like I always say, life experience will be your best-taught lesson. Now my parents, on the other hand, did not like working as much as I did, but they had no complaints when I handled things. They kept asking when I was going back to school, and my reply would be "probably never"!

I know that I could make my parents proud because I have become successful in their eyes. When my father would talk to a family member or friend on the phone, and they spoke about my career, he was optimistic. He would say, "I can see he's going to be super successful before he turns thirty, and I'm not going to discourage him." The reality was that he worked in this business and saw the kind of income potential there was for someone like me. Originally, he was not happy that I got into this business because of the direction that the financial aspect of it directed me.

How did I build connections and make friends?

My colleagues were incredible and introduced me to many up-and-coming people in different dealerships. Back in those days, social media was only transitioning from AOL Instant Messenger to MySpace. I utilized MySpace to meet people, and the birth of "Social Sher" took place years before I knew that is what people would call me.

Fitting in was a huge challenge because I chased success and had a goal to move on from mediocrity. At such a young age, 98% of the people that I met were just starting, setting themselves up for mediocrity, or just had no ambition. Make no mistake, because I did very well with the ladies, I had no problem keeping my social calendar booked when I was not at work. I guess I was truly becoming a better salesperson (lol).

This was a lesson for me to be prepared for situations where I will need to one day step up and handle things for my family. This would prove true years later when my dad lost his job, and I wrote a check almost to pay off his car. It would happen again in his final few months alive. When it all came down to it, my parents and I were always there for each other.

The biggest thing to learn here is that we need to appreciate what we have if we are blessed with a beautiful, loving family. I understand that other people are not always so lucky and suffer great pain growing up. I still believe that even in those situations, we come across great people that help lift us and inspire us. Just because the initial years have been rough, it does not mean that the result has to end unpleasantly. Also, it is important to always be networking and developing relationships.

CHAPTER 3

REACHING NEW LEVELS

My father went back to work, and things were stable. But I was missing my true home. I felt removed from my true friends and my social life. I realized that if I could make it in a brand new state that I could make it anywhere on the planet.

Living in Florida, I learned about culture shock and how different things are in other parts of the country. Selling cars was different for me in Florida, and I discovered aspects of the business that no one would teach me back home in the northeast. It was time to go back to independence and find my true happiness. I gave my two months' notice, and I finished the year selling many vehicles to make money for my move back to New Jersey.

I took a job selling Infiniti, but it did not last long. I got fired because I ran an email marketing campaign promoting a sale that my General Manager told me to run. We had over seventy Infiniti G35 vehicles in stock and needed to move some metal. He said "do what you have to do as our gloves are off". After doing that I got in trouble. Our factory district manager was not happy because it was against corporate policy. It was indeed a lesson in business compliance for me.

The good news is I was living in an area where I had connections, so finding opportunities was not challenging. I made several small moves from dealer to dealer until landing at an Acura dealership with a management title. We were a two-person Internet department taking over for the previous interment manager that only sold ten units per month. Between the two of us, we grew to thirty units per month. My partner quit her job, making me the Lone Ranger for the next eight months. I became one of the highest-paid Acura sales consultants in the region. My best month I made just shy of $16,000 delivering twenty-five units. Not bad for a twenty-three-year-old, right?

I needed help because I was working six days a week, and we had many opportunities. We hired a new partner for me to work with, and as a team, we decided to cover each other and split every deal. The result?

Thirty-five units per month with better gross and a consistent $14,000 per month for each of us. At this point, things are on the way up.

All good things have to end sometimes, right?

My General Sales Manager was an exploiter. We were so busy that I needed his help to fill out a few buyer's orders to package a deal. He decided to try to play a game of extortion with me. He sat me down one on one and told me that I should kick him back $50 for helping me on each deal. Yes, you read that right. My $140,000 per year general sales manager, that gets paid on my production wanted to extort me because I needed his help for five minutes.

I later found out that I was making as much money selling as the general sales manager, and he got sour about it. He was great at structure and process due to his military background. However, he had a lousy personality and could not even get up to help close a deal. He would send a senior salesperson to help. The guy loved to sit on the computer and convey superiority. I admit he was not bad at structuring deals, but when it came to firsthand situations, he was lacking.

The dealer had cut our advertising and hired a third person for the department. Our incomes tanked to less than half of what I was making. It was time to level up. My networking skills were developing, and I became friends with all of my vendors. I had in the industry teach me how to desk car deals and do trade appraisals. It was time to grow, and I knew it.

A huge Honda dealership recruited me by one of my friend's recommendations. The store was hitting record volume, but the internet department had one person selling twenty-five units per month, with five hundred internet leads coming in monthly. They were overlooking some serious opportunities and needed a better process. They were impressed with my numbers at the Acura dealership and offered me the position of Internet Director.

I ran a campaign hiring two more people while helping sell hands-on. I was handling advertising, desking deals, and appraising trades. Thankfully the finance department befriended me and taught me about deal structure. We were off to the races. I finally made it, twenty-four years old, with a six-figure director position of a multi-million dollar business. Nothing comes without a challenge, though, as jealousy and hatred came my way from all new car managers.

My department moved the needle, selling upwards of seventy-five units per month with only a three-person team. Our gross per unit was $400 higher than the showroom sales department. The finance department loved me because I worked the deals properly, and the contracts came into them loaded and ready to go. When a salesperson was off, I would make the sale and deliver the car to avoid losing half of their money. We had a solid team, and I learned what it is to lead. My employees were more than double my age too.

I got hot and excited to buy a home. My general manager put ideas in my head that I should buy a house. He said because I am young and successful that I should take on the responsibility, and it will build more character. At twenty-four years old, I almost bought a $300,000 house that would cost me over $2,000 per month to live in. My attorney talked me out of making the purchase, and so did my parents. It all worked out because two weeks later, my seventy car per month department that generated over $150,000 per month in gross profit was shut down.

Oddly enough, at the same time, my grandfather ended up in the hospital. I took some time to handle this issue as my parents lived across the country. The job offered me to go back on the floor and sell used cars. But no way was I going backward in my career, especially since I was a way better sales manager than the other managers. I quit this job, filed for unemployment to relax for a few months, and focused on more significant career moves.

This move created drama as this dealership ripped me off for over $6,000 in commissions from my last month working there as a manager. I had to take them to small claims court and lost due to some shady tactics that they pulled. This would not be the last time I would get ripped off, but it sure was a huge life lesson. I would learn about getting ripped off more times in the future.

I desperately wanted out of retail. The few months that I took off, I spent just enjoying my life. I reconnected with an old friend that got in the business with me, and we started taking trips to Atlantic City. I got good at blackjack, and we were taking weekly trips to go gamble. After three months, it was time to get back to work and live an everyday life.

I interviewed for a business development manager position at another Honda dealership. I got hired right on the spot! That was a wild experience that taught me about complete dealership operations and expenses. This Honda dealership was doing terribly and losing credibility with the manufacturer. They could not get validated for the president's award.

The General Manager that hired me was a powerhouse that built and ran the biggest Honda dealerships in the United States. His name is Arwin Bharaj. When I was only twenty-five years old, he took me under his wing, and together we rebuilt one of his dealerships.

My duty was to be the business development manager that also desks deals, help close customers, and fix the Honda Exel Facilitation for the dealership with every single department. We more than doubled the numbers for the BDC (Business Development Center) department from around thirty units per month to about sixty-five units. We also fixed processes in the dealership and turned them around. In sales, we were selling up to two hundred units per month for $500,000. In fixed operations, we grew our profit to over $250,000 per month.

This was a lesson in general management for me. I do not talk much about that job and the lessons that I learned. My general manager became a lifelong friend and mentor. He hired me to consult at two of his stores years later. This experience started to create the basis for my automotive consulting and training business, Dealer eTraining, that would enter the marketplace a few short years later.

We both worked at this dealership for less than a year and quit at the same time. An opportunity with a startup company came, so I moved ahead. I connected with a company called RedNumbat that served auto dealerships. It was a software company that provided easy price quoting solutions for consumers visiting automobile dealership websites.

I have to credit the founder, Joe Antley, for allowing me to be in charge of dealer relations and allowing me to be the spokesperson for this up-and-coming company. This was where I began networking with the industry and learning the who's who of the industry. I invested in conventions and conferences like National Automobile Dealers Association (NADA) and Digital Dealer. I also started writing for industry blogs and publications. Everywhere I went, I was known, and the attention that I gathered created much confidence in myself. Social media was exploding between the growth of Facebook and industry networking sites.

I got heavily involved with Automotive Digital Marketing, a major industry networking site that was built by a true automotive pioneer named Ralph Paglia. He was known as the godfather of automotive digital marketing for his lengthy resume and experience of being the first to sell cars on the internet. Ralph was a dear friend and mentored most people like myself coming up in the business. Sadly, he passed away about nine months ago as I wrote this book.

As this chapter ends, it is crucial to consider how many experiences a person can go through in a few short years. We are talking about three years where I went from getting fired as a salesperson to building and running two dealerships to becoming nationally known with a startup company! The lesson here is that we should never stop chasing our goals. Never stop chasing growth. If I could do so well in my mid-twenties, I should be able to do ten times better in my thirties. As you will learn in the next chapter, nothing in life comes easy.

When you take direct action and continue to move forward, it's incredible how far you can come in only three years. This was a time when I learned some self-discipline and to take responsibility. Until I got into management, I would go out on Friday nights and come to work hungover on Saturday morning, feeling like I had been through the wringer. While many people even in management get away with it, I stopped the minute I became a leader. I refused to look like an immature fool in front of the people I lead, and worse, look bad in front of my department heads. The self-awareness that I possessed was genuine!

When you are growing and allowed to advance, it is crucial to take it seriously. Playtime is over when it is time to be a leader and motivator. A chief commands respect because of how they conduct themselves! Be the person you want others before you to become, and you will always be one step ahead of the game.

CHAPTER 4

BAD ADVICE = MISTAKES

Let's backtrack to when I moved back from Florida to New Jersey to work at the Infiniti dealership. I did something that I considered to be a foolish move at the time. I did it to get my parents off my back about finishing college. I enrolled in an online college while working but with a focus on business management. I will not mention the school's name because I do not want to catch lawsuits for speaking the truth about what a super expensive scam that was.

The classes were easy, and after a 12-hour workday, I spent an hour a night working on lessons. It was absolute torture. I would take out a $20,000 student loan and take classes until the $20,000 was spent. I'd take six months off and pay off the $20,000 before taking a new loan. I did this until I was in for $60,000 for a degree I never completed.

Now let's fast forward to my days of working with RedNumbat and becoming known in the industry. I was young and hungry with automotive retail experience but no business-to-business expertise. I still had some immaturity in my character. I was very outspoken and told it like it is. Corporate politics and holding back was never a strong suit for me.

I made many mistakes with my character of how I expressed myself and communicated with others. If there were a disagreement, I would get into social media battles. It was not a good look for me. It hurt me because it presented me negatively to many important people that I was connecting with. At this point, I am young and full of piss and vinegar. I had earned respect from many and lost respect from some too.

Sadly, we could not get RedNumbat off the ground due to a lack of funding. We had maybe thirty dealer clients at the time. While it may look like we failed because we folded, I still believe that the experience created growth opportunities for Joe Antley and I for years to come. We both made big moves and took great jobs.

At this point, an opportunity of a lifetime came. I am twenty-seven years old and about to be employed as the eCommerce and business development director for an up-and-coming Nissan dealer in New York, making five figures per month. We will discuss this in the next chapter. But a college education was not going to be completed, as I learned two months after I took this job.

I took a class in which there was a software glitch. The software glitch prevented my work and projects from being submitted on time. My jerk college professor would not work with me and failed me. That's when the school started to play extortion with me and cancel my loans. So I got fed up and dropped out.

I decided that I was moving up without the piece of paper. I was mad that I wasted $60,000 to please my parents. I could have used that money to buy a house. Just a little over a year before that, as you can recall, I almost did.

What's the point here? You will find that many times in life, people often do not look after your best interests. Some can become a trusted source and motivate you into making a big mistake. Case in point, that general manager of the large Honda store in which I ran a seventy-five car a month internet department that generated over $200,000 per month in profit worked me to the bone and wanted to see me burn out.

Here's the other point. Even your loved ones who only want you to succeed will also try to lead you down a path that is not best for you. I lost $60,000 on a rip-off college, and I should have invested into something exceedingly more profitable like stocks or a more luxurious home in the future. At that time, pleasing my parents was more important to me.

The last point was one I did not mention earlier. I developed a personal friendship with my college advisor and financial representative that sold me on joining this fraudulent school. I felt like they were looking after my best interests, but they were earning commission to sell me on a massive scam of an education. They cost me $60,000. This was the second time I got scammed out of money.

Please understand, the only person we need to please is ourselves. College is not for everyone. I despised school. But I read books! I networked! I spent my own hard-earned money to attend conferences and rub shoulders with the big leaguer's. These things paid off the most. I know that I have as much (if not more) business, marketing, and sales knowledge as someone walking around with a college degree.

I have even more to offer. I have communication skills, and I can sell myself and my abilities. I have zero fear of rejection because I'll find a way to get into an even better opportunity. Why? The school of hard knocks and experience gave me abilities to carve out my style. I do things on my terms and not how society wants me to do them. Many will not like this and will have an opinion about it. But I promise you, the ones that understand will appreciate and give me the shot of a lifetime.

In no way am I bashing a college education. The world needs attorneys, doctors, accountants, scientists, and engineers. Some fields do require an education. The world also needs bartenders and coffee baristas that waste their time and money on useless liberal arts and psychology degrees. It's all about learning the world with an open mind and being self-aware of what your potential is. We make our choices based on our influences.

If you are young and just getting started, I want you to open your mind. I want you to think about what you want out of life. Think about what goals you want to achieve. More importantly, think about what makes you happy and go for it. But please understand your happiness can leave you either poor, average, or bring you massive amounts of success in your field. But then again, what does success mean to you?

It's not all about the money. I have made and lost lots of money. I have fallen more than once, and I came back stronger. The art of life comes in swings both upwards and downwards. While it is offensive and a miserable feeling, I can say I have zero regrets about the unfortunate times I went through. What doesn't kill you makes you stronger!

What's more important is to be careful who you surround yourself with. If you want to take your life, career, and future seriously, you should surround yourself with people that operate at higher levels than you do. If you're going to be a significant earner, you must become friends with high-income professionals and get inspired by their habits.

Please understand that you live in a world where it is every person for themselves. The world does not care about your problems. The world does not care about your bills and your debt. Sometimes the people that you think are there to help you turn around and do the opposite. So tread lightly and understand what is right and what is wrong. Learn from experiences and take matters into your own hands.

CHAPTER 5

GROWTH, REJECTION & POWER MOVES

Let's continue about this incredible new job that I took. A friend I made on social media was the managing partner of a brand new car dealership. Steve Risso and I connected, and he hired me. I will forever consider him one of the secrets of my success. He was such an influential leader. He and I reinvented automotive business development specifically for our store. He created the process to manage me and held me accountable.

This laid the groundwork for how I did things moving forward in the industry. Steve helped develop me into an effective leader. I was the eCommerce and BDC director at twenty-seven years old as I mentioned in the last chapter, I finally gave up on college two months after taking this job. My father's dreams of wearing a suit to work came true even if I did not give him a piece of paper stating I am a college graduate. By most people's standards, I was very successful and on my way up. My family and friends were proud of me and inspired by my actions.

I was not living what most people would consider everyday life. I did not work a corporate 9-5 with holidays and weekends off. I worked six days a week, open to close. My career was stressful. I was running a business development center and managing the marketing for a brand new dealership that we took from selling thirty cars to over two hundred and fifty per month in just nine months. I worked with heavy advertising budgets and intense management that demanded the best. These days that dealership sells over four hundred cars per month and is one of the top Nissan dealers in the nation. I am honored to have been a part of that experience.

I finally decided that I had become significant enough to take on new endeavors. I watched my bank and vendor reps work from home with travel making the same money without working as hard. I wanted out of retail and work for a vendor. But just like with everything else in life, I had to deal with rejection, politics, and other issues.

I would interview for a position with a marketing company that I was way more qualified for than many people they solicited. Sadly I would get passed over, and I can think of twenty companies and jobs that would do the same. Sometimes it was because I did not have a college degree. Sometimes it would be because I did not have experience selling to car dealers even though I worked for them for eight years and was involved in many decision-making. No, those things did not matter.

But I learned over the years that rejection came to me for more than just those reasons. At this point, I had started to become well known in the entire automotive industry. I was writing for magazines and blogs. I was networking and had developed significant relationships. I was now what they call a thought leader. My voice grew, and I was outspoken, and that made many fear me. They were rejecting me for being "Stan Sher."

At the time, it was depressing to contemplate. Today, I laugh about it and take great honor in knowing that I can cause that much chatter. Corporations need soldiers that will follow their agendas. They do not need someone that is outspoken and can change the game. How do I know that? Well, I worked with many unsavory vendors and marketing companies that did not align with my or my dealer's needs. To bring in someone that can influence positive change is scary and dangerous.

They will hire someone that never sold a car before over someone that genuinely can help car dealers. Unfairness like this still exists today. I meet people working for automotive vendors that have zero experience in this industry. Again companies need soldiers to follow their agendas, and our society has designed it this way. Go to college and get a degree. Go to work for a corporation to be their soldier.

I got tired of rejection, but I never gave up. I accepted an offer to show my skills and run a national training company. I was excited because BDC is precisely what I was great at doing. I traveled the country and trained car dealers on internet sales and business development. It was there where I developed business skills that made me powerful in many aspects of my life. I learned how to do public relations and public speaking. I studied recruiting talent to join my team, and I taught myself how to network and create strategic alliances. And more importantly, I learned how to market myself. This opportunity transformed me and made me into what I am today.

Because of who I was working for, I also developed bad habits. I created the habit of being defensive if criticized by others. I watched the CEO of the company act in ways that were inappropriate internally and with fellow business professionals. I quickly took the good and the bad. Sadly the unpleasant things I learned added to my character. It would take me another five years to break free of the negativity.

We had a situation where our CEO got into a jet ski accident when he was out of the country. I ran his multimillion-dollar company for three months while he was on his death bed. I saved him and his family from losing everything they had built. In return, I dealt with disrespect and ridicule from him. I got a pay raise that was a complete joke. The final moment for me was when we put on a seminar for car dealers. He showed me contempt on day two of the event, so I walked out and quit my job right before I was supposed to go up on stage to speak for the very first time in my life.

One month later, I opened up my own training firm, Dealer eTraining. I had become his competition, and I took the market by storm. He went to war with me to diminish my brand and image. He was afraid because I could expose him for his shortcomings. We had social media battles and even court battles. It all ended in nothing. We just do not talk or communicate anymore.

Slander like this was another example of how much harder I had to work to achieve any success. It took me six months to land my first client and first speaking opportunity at a conference. I went on a two-year run, training dealers and speaking at conferences. I continued to market myself through social media and magazines. I was doing everything as a one person show. I also made plenty of mistakes because of the bad habits my previous CEO taught me. It would take me years to outgrow those mistakes and prove to the industry that I serve where my heart is.

There were significant rises and even bigger falls over the next five years. Amid my growth and success, this previous CEO, along with a few other colleagues, went on social media and destroyed my name. I experienced a lot of slander and backstabbing. My business suffered greatly. I lost over $300,000 of business opportunities, and many connections turned away from associating with me. I was part of the problem because I was aggressively being defensive and tackled the issue head-on.

The result was a loss of business revenue and ultimately going broke. I got evicted from my luxury apartment and destroyed my credit. This was only eight years ago as I wrote this book. I was living in an area too close to this competitor that caused me problems. Those were some very dark times for me. One thing to note is that I never succumbed to developing bad personal habits. I never drank, and I never did drugs. I just lived my life and worked to get back on top.

In the coming chapters, you will learn my strategy for getting back on track, and I hope this is a lesson that serves people well. I moved back to my home area and humbled myself. I took some small social media clients that helped cover basic costs while going back to work. It was time to go silent and focus on the rebirth of my name and reputation.

Albert Einstein once said that "A person who never made a mistake never tried anything new." I was not going to be that person! I applied for a corporate job outside of automotive that allowed me to work from home. This job taught me new industries such as big-box retail and flooring. I was a sales trainer and field manager for an entire territory working with a major home construction chain and the flooring company. I worked on this team for almost two years before being transferred to work with our pre-paid wireless division. There I would also spend over two years as a field manager for a large territory.

The money was very light, but the flexibility of the job allowed me to be a hustler. I got recruited by a dealer group opening up a brand new independent dealership in New Jersey as part of their national expansion. I was the General Sales Manager with a low six-figure pay plan and their first employee in this dealership. They bought a failing dealership that struggled to sell eight cars per month. In my first month with zero advertising and operating under the old dealership, we sold twenty-six vehicles for slightly over $70,000 gross profit.

I had only two salespeople and a finance manager. We had a service department that I would eventually also oversee. The store would grow to sell around seventy units per month for over $250,000 in gross profit. My service department was also cracking $100,000 per month. I had one problem. We kept the previous owner on the payroll as part of the buy-sell, and he held his office.

The man that failed as a dealer stayed with the new store. He kept making calls to my boss and constantly throwing me under the bus. He did not like how I was appraising vehicles and complained about how I stepped up on trades. It is funny how I ran $3,000 per unit when I did that too. I mean $350,000 per month profit at a store that was losing over $100,000 before me. I saw no more growth for me and got tired of the nonsense, and left the job shortly before I completed a full year. I utilized the skills that I learned seven years earlier when we transformed that Honda dealership.

At the same time, I kept working my corporate job. It was six and seven day weeks for me as I fixed my credit and put money in the bank. I was making six figures again, and life got great again. I found my happiness again. All I did was duplicate what I did in my early years when I worked three jobs and went to school! I did it on a much higher level with a much higher income.

I learned that mistakes are forgiven because the truth always comes out, and people will see you for what you are. I am proud that I have always been faithful to myself and remain outspoken.

Suppose I'm not too fond of something; I will speak out about it. For instance, politics does not apply to me because I do not take sides. I am opinionated, but It comes from my life experience. Talk to me about marketing, social media, google analytics, and SEO (search engine optimization), and we will have an intelligent conversation. Talk to me about desking a car deal or managing a sales team, and we will also have a scholarly discussion. I made it a point to know my business and be good at a little bit of everything, and just enough to be deadly.

As I said before, life will have swings both up and down. The rollercoaster of life brings many experiences and develops our authentic characters. You have not truly lived unless you dealt with rejection in the highest forms. How you come back, and the power moves you make will determine how you will end up.

By the way, that corporate job afforded me to save up money and buy my first home. Imagine losing everything from your apartment to lots of money and work and coming back more vital than ever. Four years after things went terrible, I bought a home and two cars. How? I knew how to maneuver situations, and I outworked everyone else! If you do it once, you can do it again!

When I say that I can talk about all of these subjects, it's because I made it a point to become the jack of all trades. I keep thinking about my friend Ralph Paglia who I mentioned earlier in this book. I think even they left the automotive industry and came back better than ever. My father used to tell me that any experience that I can get is one more step to survival in this scary world. He used to talk about that when I was learning how to drive a manual transmission car. He would say "imagine one day you need to drive a truck and unlike many other people you know how to drive a stick…well son guess who gets the job?" He was right!

After leaving my General Sales Manager position, I kept getting calls to fix business development centers in local dealerships. At one point, I was consulting three dealerships full time. I also became a facilitator for a major manufacturer, taking on a forty-day consulting project. The damage done to my name by my competitor did not matter anymore, and I got my rhythm back. In fact, that competitor exposed their true colors by burning bridges. Many unfollowers and naysayers came back trying to be my friend and apologizing to me. A very rich and successful man once told me "The shit always rises to the top" meaning that if you stay in the game long enough the truth will always come out.

CHAPTER 6

THE ADVENTURES OF SOCIAL SHER

Let's again go back a few years to before I went broke. I guess we can call them the original golden years. I am trying to become a leading authority in the automotive industry, and I do not realize I am good at social media. One of the most brilliant minds I ever met in marketing and a friend, Brian Pasch, once said I should become "Social Sher" and leverage it into something. It took me three years to decide what to do with it.

At this point, I am an entrepreneur with a million ideas. I had been doing Dealer eTraining for a total of three years, and I'm just getting by making a small living, similar to being a manager at a car dealership.

My friend is a colossal VP for a multilevel marketing company in dire need of social media, marketing, and branding services. I made a game plan for how to help him with other divisions of his company. I decided to take my experience of how I got known in the automotive industry and duplicate it for them.

Just like that, "Social Sher" was born, and I had a high four-figure a month business with eight clients that were all partners. We focused on helping them with recruiting staff, creating a positive social media image, blogging, and creating press releases to give each office brand awareness in their respective communities. Our challenge was due to the nature of their business, and they were constantly getting a bad image online. Reputation management was the focus of marketing at the time, and we did everything to improve their appearance on search engines.

Our results increased recruiting efforts by 25% and retention of associates increased by 40%. Eventually, the admins of the offices learned our practices and decided to keep what we do in-house, retaining "Social Sher" as a marketing consultant and coach for many years. It was a time when social media management gurus were popping up everywhere. I kept it small and personable because my main business was "Dealer eTraining," while "Social Sher" was still a side hustle.

Let's fast forward to after I came back strong working a corporate job and building a dealership.

A follower and fan of mine in automotive reached out to me and wanted to partner up on social media for car dealers. We partnered up and became an entire agency. We would take a brand new Mitsubishi dealer to a deep level of visibility on social media. Our focus was on the inventory and the culture of the dealership. Too many marketing and public relations firms focus on useless, bland, generic social media posts that deliver zero value to their clients.

We broke the trends and the rules. We were as accurate, and no hands barred as it gets. Our choice was to work with dealers with an internal culture showcased beautifully on social media. We also needed the dealership to have the most remarkable cars. Let's face it! We want to help sell more cars. We want to help service more cars. No one cares about the local nonsense these fake gurus wish to promote.

Our services included graphic designs, memes, press releases, web design, lead generation, and video marketing. Social Sher became a spokesperson for clients to do videos professionally in one take and deliver a lasting impression. Social Sher is what I have become, and I was able to do the things for our clients that they were afraid to do. Many people fear the camera and cannot naturally speak when filming. I started to film promotional content for every aspect of the dealership. I also would interview staff members at the stores.

We grew on to build a massive brand for a Mitsubishi dealership and its General Manager at one point. We turned the general manager into a mini local celebrity through social media, video marketing, and press releases. The demand grew, and we serviced many new and independent dealerships in New York and New Jersey. It was inspiring when people would say to me, "hey, I saw you on YouTube," when I walked into a store. I used this as fuel to empower me to push myself even further. Speaking of Mitsubishi, we were on their radar as we did unique social media work successfully for multiple Mitsubishi dealers.

Sometimes partnerships are not meant to last. My ex-partner is a great guy and an incredible camera person. He is detail-oriented and among the best, I worked with. When it comes to cars, he is an encyclopedia. We developed some excellent skills together. But our visions did not align. We still talk these days. He does his thing, and I do mine.

I later went solo as Social Sher and expanded to small businesses. I helped a significant salon called "City Master Barbers" with two locations in central New Jersey with marketing, branding, and business consulting. The owner of the salon is a great personal friend that I also look up to. If we talk about brilliance and the perfect example of running a beauty business in a highly competitive marketplace, take a look at this brand.

I even worked with a guitar string cleaning company helping elevate the brand through YouTube and Instagram. At times, businesses bring me in to consult on marketing strategy and create a branding game plan. I duplicated my consulting process from Dealer eTraining and brought it to Social Sher. We even worked with a chamber of commerce in Florida and provided public relations services.

So while this may have sounded like a sales pitch for marketing services, let me assure you that this is not a pitch at all. I want you to understand that serious points stem from the adventures of Social Sher. I made big investments and bigger mistakes by thinking I can run it all. In order to be a successful it is important to build a solid team.

Here is the lesson that I am preaching.

I mentioned earlier about learning different aspects of business and marketing. I also said how much self-education and experiences I put myself through. The lesson here is, we can take life experiences and create a business opportunity from them. I was not happy that one business was making me a living. An opportunity came to take my skill sets to the next level and start a second business.

There are many benefits of entrepreneurship on multiple levels that are very rewarding. I'm not just talking about tax benefits, either. It is rewarding to do for others what you have done for yourself and then monetize it. I took what I was great at and what I truly enjoyed from the heart and turned it into multiple six-figure businesses. Let me assure you that life is not dull when you are busy and have priorities. Life is not unhappy when you have relationships that allow you to make a great living.

When one business slows down, you have the other business keeping you busier than ever. It is a blessing. I learned in my teens when I was a lifeguard that it's essential to have more than one income. I worked two lifeguarding jobs and ran a side hustle teaching swimming lessons. That's how I paid for my brand new car, college tuition, cell phone bill, social life, and saved money while in school and living at home. You become what your life experiences have taught you to become.

You are about to learn how I failed again and experienced even more significant falls. Once again, I went back to basics and built myself up to where I am today. Bill Gates said it best when he said, "To win big, you sometimes have to take big risks." Well, I took significant risks, and it hurt heavily, but I persevered! As Elton John sang, "I'm still standing after all this time."

CHAPTER 7

THE POWER OF FIVE

Theodore Roosevelt, who was our nation's twenty-sixth president and also the youngest president in history, once said that "It is hard to fail, but It is worse never to have tried to succeed." The process of trying is beautiful, and the process of failing, while it may seem perilous, is actually where we get proper schooling.

The difference between failure and success is what you do with your power of five. If you cannot leverage these five things, you will fail. If I lost everything today and had no way to buy groceries tomorrow or pay my bills, I would use the power of five and bring myself out of poverty within six months.

Here is what I would do:

1. Become an Uber & Lyft driver. I would quickly sign up for all the programs. I would set up my primary vehicle and get to work. If I do four solid hours, I can make $100 in one day. Now I can buy gas and groceries. At five days a week, I'll make at least $500 a week. That's a start.

2. I update my resume, and I spend three hours per day searching for a job in my field(s) that includes sales, marketing, management, and training. My goal is to apply to twenty jobs minimally per day. These jobs will pay no less than $80,000 per year with benefits.

3. I spend two hours a day speaking to my contacts and connections to carve out an opportunity.

4. I would spend three hours working on rebuilding my business. I change my marketing plans, and I start prospecting companies. I might land five clients that I can work with, and perhaps I might not even need to take a corporate job. Maybe I land only one or two clients that I can work with as a side hustle while working my full-

time job. It allows me to stop driving Uber and Lyft and focus on my growth. After all, sitting in a car for four hours nonstop is not fun. I have been there and done that.

5. I would make sure that I maintain a smile and a positive attitude. I must be pragmatic and provide a great aura with every communication.

Twenty job applications per day at seven days a week is one hundred and forty applications per week. If you land 10% of that as interviews, you now have fourteen opportunities. Someone will offer you a job. You will be working within two weeks, depending on the onboarding process. Keep driving the car and buying groceries, and paying minimum bills. Keep talking to connections. Keep focusing on business opportunities and prospecting.

When and if it all falls apart for you, the focus should be to work the power of five every single day, seven days a week. You work it like you work a full-time job. You cannot afford to stop for a minute. This process is where the massive action that you take will convert you into an overnight success.

One of the most important steps is having great people around you. I am talking about extraordinary people that lift you and will do what they can to help you. For example, one of my best friends is Akram Ali. He saved my life when I ran out of money and had to cover an emergency. Here is another person who inspires me with a "come up" story that should be a book within itself. Akram never let me fail. We have taken care of each other in times of need with every aspect of life. Akram Ali is my brother, just like Christopher Haas.

I guarantee you that this strategy will put you back on track within a few months. Work the process for at least one year and focus on growth. You now have multiple opportunities to work with and be able to choose which one to grow with.

But Stan, how is it possible?

It's possible because my second failure gave me this experience. I did this exact strategy. I made bad business decisions and was forced to start over. I was getting back to doing Dealer eTraining and Social Sher. I took a few bad clients that ripped me off in one month for a combined sum of $15,000 in one month!

My corporate job was making changes and laid many of us off, including myself. I found myself with no income and trying to chase the money that clients ripped off. At this point, I have a hefty mortgage and two car payments. I was also living an above-average lifestyle. A few rough months, and I was behind on my mortgage payments and cars.

Most people would be completely ashamed to write about these experiences, especially when they are branding themselves. As for myself, I love telling the story because I would not be the man I am today in business and my personal life. I was going through times, but I was not afraid! When you know what you are doing, you can indeed survive and thrive!

I drove Uber and Lyft for three months. The first month I was looking for a job, I drove four hours a day. While I applied for many jobs, I was able to land an appointment with one phone call. In the second and third months, I was working a full-time six-figure job managing a car dealership and driving Uber and Lyft just to pay off debt faster. After the third month, I picked up two clients for social media while still working my job, and I quit driving Uber and Lyft.

It gets better. After only two months, my employer stabbed me in the back. It was a brand new store that a friend of mine opened up. I started building up his Kia dealership with advertising and a BDC department. One Saturday he randomly just fired me and then proceeded to rip me off for two days pay. It was not painful at this time. Remember I am recovering from a setback so this is part of the process.

At the same time, I landed a big consulting gig that paid off two of my credit cards from one week worth of work. Now I'm in the groove hustling away. I still needed a job though. I got recruited for a better job that I worked for the entire year. In my off time, I slowly rebuilt my business on the side. I paid off $30,000 of debt in eight months while living a higher standard of living again and paying my everyday living expenses.

The tenacity of my actions indeed sprung me ahead. But if it were not for my ability to communicate fearlessly, I would fail! I learned that I must turn my experiences into a story worth telling! I sell my knowledge every chance I can get. Even when I was driving Lyft, I was networking because you never know what connection you'll make. My ability to build rapport and be liked also helped me get great tips.

There's no fear after adversity hits a few times. It's just all about going back to basics. Someone will need you and will have an opportunity. But unless you put yourself out there, nothing will ever happen. If you are reading is and are currently afraid to get social and put yourself out in the public I am here to tell you to stop that nonsense. Go brand yourself and develop opportunities that will bring you success!

Here I am a few years later, and the business world has served me well. I am blessed to write about the power of five to inspire the reader. At this point, I started my third hustle and went back to doing what I did in the past with social media and sales training. My phone rings with opportunities every week for something. Why? The power of five!

CHAPTER 8

NEW BALANCE & FAMILY TRAGEDY

I spent an entire year working at that car dealership, where I went back to basics. I made less money than I was worth. I put in a lot of hours and covered the backs of many people. This was humbling and a way to prove that I am still outstanding at this. We sold a lot of cars. It was one of the best stores I ever worked for in my career. I have to thank my friend and neighbor Michael Lasko for giving me the opportunity, as he will never know how much he helped me come back up.

I rebuilt my business slowly, gathering some clients, and started building my comfort zone. I was honestly mentally tired of this full-time job, and it felt like, at this point, I was selling myself short. A conflict developed at this job where no one disclosed that I had to answer to a certain somebody. This person and I were both at the same level when it came to skills in the BDC. She was there for fifteen years and had the title of "Marketing Director". We were very competitive and she realized that I am not in it to be doing this forever due to my background. She and I got along on a personal level but battled on a business level. This drove me away eventually and I am happy that it did just that.

I slowly got myself in the groove to connect with my network and look for a move up. There was no shortage of opportunities. I even turned down a few effective options. My life was getting balanced, and so was my personal life. I got into a serious relationship with the love of my life. She moved in with me. We evened each other out and have been a rock for one another since the first day we started living together. I was working very hard to support our household.

But now we had a whole new set of problems develop. Like I mentioned earlier, my father's health was deteriorating. He stopped working and was diagnosed with liver cancer. I spent every day off from work going to my parent's house and taking care of them. We had hospital and doctor visits every week. I took care of all their groceries and started to manage their bills.

Finally, I had to put focus on my dad's last days. I was encouraged to leave my job. I took care of my dad for ten days every day until he ultimately passed away. I found myself with only a little bit of money. I had two households and two mortgages to support. Then the Covid-19 pandemic hit right after my mother, and I put my father to rest. Masks became the thing, and our world shut down. I took off two months to grieve while taking care of my sick mother multiple times per week. I was looking for a new balance.

An opportunity came back as my good friend Tom Esposito of Dealer Retention Services recruited me to be the chief operating officer for his outsource business development call center that serves car dealers. I would manage a national company with thirty employees overseeing all aspects of the business. Tommy put my extensive trade skills to good use. I did sales, marketing, recruiting, training and planning. I ran all operations and industry relations for the company.

I was also out training dealers and traveling around the country as things opened up. I got busy, and I hustled to support two households. Every single Sunday was my day to take care of my mom. We hired a private pay home attendant, and I paid for more than six months until she got approved for government assistance. I had a lot on my shoulders, and I managed to step up and come back strong.

I expanded Dealer eTraining to partner with Pay Here Marketing, where I provide my services to Buy Here Pay Here dealers. This was a new challenge as I invested time into learning how the business model works. I created a training curriculum for sales professionals that is unique to that industry. There is so much untapped potential for BHPH dealers to improve their marketing and sales efforts. I want to be the person that wakes them up! This part of the business has far less competition than when I work with retail automobile dealerships.

I got engaged to my girlfriend. We got two cats and a dog. Our home life is fantastic and full of love. I got my mother situated and took care of her to have the charge and support she needed. I left my Chief Operating Officer job to be focused on what makes me happy, training and developing people and businesses. Too many times, the calls come in with opportunities, but they are often a distraction that prevents you from achieving the greatness that you are capable of achieving. I love my friend Tom with all my heart. I'd walk through fire for that man.

But while the opportunity was not right for me, there was so much great to come out of it. It took me out of the depression that I got into after my dad passed away. It got my mind right, and I became a beast at my craft again! I will never forget this opportunity as long as I live. In fact, Tommy said that to me when we parted ways. Dealer Retention Services remains a partner of Dealer eTraining, where we refer clients that need outsourced business development services.

Everything happens for a reason. Many people give up when things get bad. I like to believe that I use past experiences to bring me back up because I know the secret code to what makes me successful. I became a better investor of my time and money too. These days I read more books and watch more inspirational videos on YouTube to set my mindset correctly. If you cannot exercise your mind, you will not move forward in life!

Once I had my fire back, I was like Leroy in the movie "The Last Dragon" in his final fight when he claimed the glow. The confidence comes back along with a big smile bringing a burning desire to make a huge comeback. There I was, working night and day, building a profitable future.

CHAPTER 9

ANOTHER VENTURE?

What do you know?

I opened a third and fourth business venture too. Sometimes distractions become opportunities. This hustle is just excellent because it's incredible how much word-of-mouth business comes. As I write this, the company has been around for ten months and has slowly produced five figures. This is without advertising and branding in full force. The name of the new brand is JSBC Associates.

I was introduced to credit repair. I got fascinated with fixing my credit at first. A multi-level marketing company approached me to start a business. What better time to improve people's credit than after a worldwide pandemic destroyed people's finances, right?

Well, I invested thirty minutes per day to watch YouTube videos and read about credit and credit repair. I studied every aspect of his credit works and became knowledgeable. I realized this multi-level marketing company is complete garbage, and the payout is a complete joke. However, I was interested in seeing what we could do with this.

Next, I invested in the following software and resources. After telling some friends, I picked up close to thirty clients that have been referring to business. It's a nice little side "hustle" that I will sit late at night and work on. I love it. It is quick money, but when I look at monthly updates and see my client's scores are up to forty to one hundred, it is rewarding.

It is a lot of fun to do something that helps people Improve their finances so that they can buy homes and automobiles. This business also taught me life skills that I wish I learned back in school. We would all live much more successful lives if these basics were taught to us during our developmental years. When I speak to potential customers and sell our services it is incredible to be able to share educational knowledge with them.

This is where I have been able to implement everything that I have ever experienced. My automotive sales background made it easy to understand credit. My marketing background has given me the ability to get the business known and seen. My training background has given me the ability to speak comfortably and provide education on the topic of credit. I also had fixed my own credit from damages in the past.

Again this is an example of how life experiences can lead to something new, fresh and exciting. Never in a million years did I think I would enter the credit repair industry. We get referrals from car dealerships and real estate agents constantly. I am able to tap into my network to build a business from the ground up.

So what is the fourth business, Stan?

The teaching opportunity here is that the more that we do and the more incredible people that we connect with the more chances at success are available. Life is about building opportunities and taking them further. We talked in the beginning that everything I ever achieved was a struggle. It doesn't matter if you are terrible at taking tests. It does not matter if you were born with a disability. It does not matter if you came from a great childhood or a bad one. In the end what matters is what you do with what shows up in front of you.

John Lennon once said that "Life Is What Happens When You're Busy Making Other Plans". Those words are so true! I had no plans to start a credit repair business just like I had no plans to get back into a social media marketing business. I made plans to go back to my core element with Dealer eTraining. Look what happened now. Now all three are working hand in hand. I am at my very best when I am incredibly busy because it gives me fulfillment and purpose.

Every single one of us at one point or another has had some form of opportunity. Only a small fraction of us actually took a shot because we get so bogged down with the negativity! I challenge you to open your mind, study every opportunity and find what you are good at and turn it into happiness and success!

CHAPTER 10

THE SKILLS THAT PAY THE BILLS

Anyone that knows me has heard me use these words many times as part of my discussions. Remember that I was not confident growing up. Remember that my grades were average or below average in school. Remember that it took me three tries to get my driver's license on the written exam.

I have my share of flaws, and I am not afraid to admit them! In fact, I am so proud of my shortcomings as I look back to where I have been in this extraordinary life. Even Lady Gaga once said that "I allow myself to fail. I allow myself to break. I'm not afraid of my flaws'. Our flaws are what make us what we are!

Since we have flaws, let us focus on our strengths and capitalize on them. I was not born great at selling. I knew nothing about marketing. However, I fell in love with it when I realized that this is how I would pay my bills.

How do you become great at selling?

How do you develop sales skills?

We are born with them even if we do not realize it. Whenever we need to get someone to see our point of view, we sell them. Sales are nothing more than communication and the transfer of energy. When people tell me they cannot sell, I tell them that they need to stop lying to themselves.

As soon as you realize that you are not afraid of what the other party says and that you can come up with a response, you are officially a salesperson. The only stopping people from being effective in sales is their fear.

The next fear of moving forward is being scared of being in front of a camera or the public. Look, our smartphones and computers are recording us. Privacy no longer exists in the year 2021. So what are you afraid of?

I know. People are afraid of the negative attention that comes from bullies. We are naturally worried about what people think. I was like that for many years. Once the situation becomes a matter of life or death, we forget about caring what people think, and we focus on what is essential.

This chapter is important because I want you to study the art of sales and marketing. I want you to read books, attend seminars and watch youtube videos. Let us get immersed in the two most important things in life to grow our careers, incomes, and businesses. Learn how to take life experiences (good or bad) and turn them into a story like what you are currently reading.

If you are making $50,000 per year but want to make $70,000, the only thing stopping you is the fear of failure. What happens if you fail the job interview? You learn from mistakes and learn how to communicate better to sell yourself better next time.

Do you know how many people I have met in positions of authority that make six and seven figures that I questioned how they got there? They got there because they possess the ability to communicate. The ability to communicate is the ability to sell. This is the number one quality that merely all successful people have.

What other skills pay the bills, Stan?

If you work in a manual labor position as a technician, plumber, construction worker, beauty industry, or anything else that involves using hands and physical activities, then those are the skills. A master barber/stylist can make $100,000 per year because they attract many clients with excellent work. A great plumber or construction worker can make millions of dollars because of their skills. There is a reason why not everyone can fix a sink or cut hair. It is a developed skill with much time and money invested in the craft.

But what else do these people possess?

Once again...sales and marketing!

A plumber or construction worker needs excellent marketing skills to be seen to generate business opportunities. Once they are in front of their prospects, they need to communicate effectively and sell the value in their time, skills, and efforts to command top dollar. A barber markets themselves with how good they look and how they are talking to their customers. They control how much of a tip they will get in the end and upsell more products and services.

It all comes down to communication skills that turn into sales and marketing skills. If we cannot establish this, we will always be controlled by others in positions of authority instead of managing our destiny. The sad thing is that we are not taught this in school.

We go out into this world unprepared to tackle the real challenges.

How do I sell?

I can turn this discussion into a whole book. For now, let us outline a simple game plan.

Step 1. Establish what you are going to offer to the marketplace. Is it a service or a product? Are we selling pens, power washing for decks, empanadas, or even a resume writing service? Master the craft!

Step 2. Get out of your comfort zone. Forget that anyone is watching you and put it out there. Some will love it and become raving fans, while others will become "haters." So what? Do they pay your bills? Get out on social media and start posting. Even if you have no idea what you are doing, start practicing. So many lessons on YouTube. No excuses why you cannot learn some of these techniques.

Step 3. Attract something irresistible to everyone that you meet. If you make terrific empanadas and always visit specific locations, why not let everyone around you know? The next thing you know, if they like the product, they will pay you, and you can sell 100 empanadas every time. This is how I built my social media business. We created some graphics and made an excellent video. We promoted it powered by the business. Next thing you know, we got leads.

Step 4. Have a passion for what you do! Get excited about what you are offering and get excited about seeing other people enjoying the product or service! The passion creates the sales pitch because you transfer your energy to the person in front of you.

Step 5. This passion and energy develops into excellent communication skills. Now that it is here, it is time to start duplicating it thousands and millions of times over. When you speak with passion you are transferring positive energy to the person that you are speaking with.

Step 6. Do not be a fraud! Everything needs to be done ethically! Every part of the business needs to be done right. If something does not work for someone, do not jam it down their throats. This can lead to reputation problems and hurt marketing for the future.

Step 7. Generate referrals and interest from friends and family of the customers. Ask for the opportunity. Sometimes the most significant revenue is made from volume.

Step 8. Continue to educate yourself to grow sales and marketing skills while repeating the first seven steps every single time.

Step 9. Take all the skills that you learned and profited with and use them to the best of your ability. Something like a life skill and a learned business skill when combined will make you a powerful individual.

Step 10. Work two and three jobs and hustles until the hustle becomes the main income. How else can we learn and try to improve ourselves?

Step 11. Do not fear rejection! Stop being afraid! People live their entire lives being afraid of what happens if they are told "No". If told "No" then ask questions and build value. Find out why something is not working for them. If there is no solution then move on! You must understand that everyone you meet will have a different personality. I always like to say, "there's an ass for every seat" because it is true!

While this was a quick crash course, we elaborate in a coaching or training session and turn these simple eight steps into a whole day or week-long discussion.

I believe that we need to learn basic language skills to read and write. We need to learn how to count.

We also need to learn a bit about history so that we can develop intelligence through discussion. But among everything we need to teach communication skills. I highly recommend that everyone join a Toastmasters chapter in your area where you will network with like minded people and together become competent communicators through public speaking. You move to another level as a person and as a professional by going through this journey.

We all have skills that make us great. Turn a positive hobby into a revenue generating operating business. Learn how to generate opportunities through communication and networking.

In fact there's so many opportunities to become a networker through meetups and networking groups. Meetup.com is a powerful one to join. I have been actively involved in networking groups for different industries that I have been able to serve. You will find it fascinating how these groups almost always can lead to growth.

My life experiences of working multiple jobs and the love of the process gave me the skills to survive and thrive in the bad times. My sales skills selling automobiles and dealing with businesses gave me the ability to sell anything to anyone. My experience working as a trainer for a training company taught me how to train people but also the different avenues of marketing. I had to brand myself into an opportunity. The automobile sales experience pushed me to know about credit and how to fix it because I knew what to look for. Experience is the most important tool to build the skills to pay the bills. Learn to take experiences and create from it.

I still believe that the fear or rejection is something that we all need to work on within ourselves. When we stop being afraid of communication with people we naturally become great. The greatness within us comes when we free ourselves of being afraid and we go out and chase accomplishments.

CHAPTER 11

THE FINAL WORDS OF WISDOM

Our world is starting to come back, and the future is bright for those that will utilize the power of five. As I write this, we live through historical times that have created new structures to live our lives. This new start is a fresh opportunity to change the game and do something huge. The one thing to understand is that you are in charge of the result of the actions that you take.

Please understand that as you grow, more people will want and need something from you. Others will always want to piggyback on your success. Sponging often happens when they cannot put themselves out there the same way that you did. For example, I cannot tell you how many people want me to be a reseller for their products and services to car dealerships. People forget that I also need help getting clients and growing my own business, but they distract me with their needs. It is normal and will happen more often when you make multiple connections.

I leave money on the table by not involving myself in these distractions. But here is the thing. If I start being a reseller for some other brand, my message can get lost, and the focus of what I am trying to achieve will go to someone else's business. Always remember that you are your brand, and you must focus on your accomplishments. No one wants to help you build yours, but they will gladly use you for themselves and take advantage.

If you must become an employee, understand that your employer will try to own you and control you at their own will. It isn't easy to go back from entrepreneur to employee because now you have an entrepreneur mindset. However, if you become so good and in demand, you can know you're worth and keep some control. But know that you are on their payroll, so you must deliver and do a great job.

More importantly, Our society fills our minds with the need to follow a specific plan. An objective that works out for some but often disappointments many. The program is to go to school, make the honor roll and end up in college with a lot of debt. What once had a much higher success rate has steadily declined into a higher failure rate.

Think about this. How many people end up doing what they said they wanted to do when they grow up? How many do you know?

Look at the times we are in and look at what takes over our lives. Many people cannot think for themselves and require social proof. To get accepted, people worry about what others think. People are losing or not attaining practical communications skills that lead them to go out and get what they want in life.

We see many people adhering to the rules of society that create a "scared" mindset. The "scared" perspective makes people afraid to take risks that put them on a challenging journey. I am talking about the arduous journey that has high reward potential in overall life.

I have seen so many people become lazy because things are way too easy. These days in kids' sports, everyone gets a trophy just for participating, even if they did not win. What are we promoting? We are announcing that it is ok to lose? Well, I'm here to tell you that it is NOT ok to fail. In the battle of life, we have responsibilities that include taking care of others that depend on us. We have bills to pay.

Does your mortgage company or landlord forgive and reward you if you fail at earning an income to pay your bills next month? NO!

Before you start to think that I am insensitive here, I want you to think about losing as an opportunity to grow. If we lose something, does it mean life is over? No! Tomorrow is a new day. Start with a fresh mindset and be prepared to learn from your mistakes. Analyze what could have been done differently and create a new plan and how you can improve.

We need to start raising the next generation of people to take life seriously. We need to instill in them traditional values like an excellent work ethic. We need to develop people to be interested in things that can guide them into a positive future. We need to go back and condition ourselves to act like this.

Where does it begin? It starts with our surroundings and environment. When we operate a certain way, we develop a culture. That culture is what I was a part of, and that is what created this story.

Also, we all need to develop an abundant mindset. Learn to live life on your terms. It is too often that we worry about losing something that we never had. When you attain "skills that pay the bills," you can control the situation, and you can fight adversity. I have faced so much rejection in my life that even with the pain of it, I move on to bigger and better things.

Adversity comes in many forms. Some are born with challenges, while others come from challenging situations. To come up from limited resources and build "skills that pay the bills" is a beautiful thing. That discussion is the purpose of this book.

Through the process of life, we will incur many scars. Scars heal and should make us stronger every single time. The wounds hurt and can feel like they are never-ending. But it is how we come back up from them and heal that matters most.

Whenever I wake up before I even open my eyes, I say a blessing for everything that I have gone through in my life. Every experience, mistake, obstacle, generous act & "NO" is what made me the man that I am today. I am here to tell you that the process of growth is a beautiful one. Please take a moment every day to reflect on where you come from and look forward to the coming success. It takes work. It takes a positive mindset. It takes surrounding yourself with beautiful people that uplift you.

Each of us will have to make this decision. A dear friend and automotive industry colleague whom I also consider a mentor, James Ziegler's "The Alpha

Dawg," talks about the ultimate decision. He decided that "I will be a success" after he started over again. He finishes the statement where he says that five years later, he was a millionaire. He has said these words the same way hundreds of times, and I still get inspired every time I hear them in his speeches. I made the same decision as well. Make a decision that you will become a success and take action to get there. If you fail, then try again until you get it right!

I hope that this book inspired you to take action and to continue growing. Our society needs a wake-up call. There are plenty of people that are missing key elements that hold them back from surviving and thriving. Use this message in good health and prosper. I will see you at the top!

ABOUT STAN

Stan Sher is an automotive industry thought leader and sales trainer. Stan spent eight years building a successful career in the automotive retail sector, starting as a high-performing sales professional and growing into high-level executive management roles. After successfully being a part of a fast-growing Nissan dealership in New York where breaking records was the name of the game, he became a world wide trainer and consultant for car dealerships.

He is the founder of Dealer eTraining, a training and consulting company that improves internet sales, business development, and marketing operations for auto dealerships. He is also an author for most major industry publications and a speaker at conferences.

Due to his marketing and branding ability, he later started Social Sher, a social media and public relations firm that serve various industries by building brands and generating visibility for businesses struggling to get ahead in these turbulent times. They create graphics, videos, and unique content to engage. Stan is also the founder of JSBC Associates, a minor credit repair and financial literacy education firm that helps people repair, build and establish their credit and manage it effectively.

Stan came from an Eastern European background moving to the united states at age five with his family. This is why he maintains a lot of old-school traditions from how he was raised. When not working and splitting his time between the different ventures, he can be found playing guitar that includes a collection of twelve guitars. He is a huge music lover and attends concerts every chance he gets. He also loves to cook and entertain. He is called Social Sher because he loves people and to be around people, always building relationships and helping people as much as he can. Stan is a family man that consists of a beautiful fiancé, Jennifer, and three pets (2 cats and a dog).

Being open to connections, he invites you to reach out to him by visiting http://www.stansher.net

www.ingramcontent.com/pod-product-compliance
Lightning Source LLC
Chambersburg PA
CBHW060341130626
46553CB00003B/1077